SARAJEVO ROSES

T0159821

SARAJEVO ROSES

RORY WATERMAN

CARCANET

First published in Great Britain in 2017 by
CARCANET PRESS LTD
Alliance House, 30 Cross Street
Manchester M2 7AQ
www.carcanet.co.uk

A CIP catalogue record for this book is available
from the British Library: ISBN 9781784104085.

Design: Luke Allan.
Printed and bound in England by SRP Ltd.

The publisher acknowledges financial assistance
from Arts Council England.

CONTENTS

SARAJEVO ROSES

Mapless – but anyway I sought the Iron Age fort
as air flung pompoms of mistletoe
in the apple trees up from the church; then
a kestrel was picking the thrust and stall of wind
above a lifeless field of waterlogged clods
(starlings had poured to a tuft in the mesh of hedge);
and next a copse, instant and dense,
hid a gap-toothed plough then behind it, dotting a clearing,
earth-caked pheasant feeders, by a downed once-electric fence
where KEEP OUT PRIVATE was nailed in high on a trunk;
tall beech saplings juddered, irate at each top,
and burnished leaves rotted in unflustered piles.
And here was the buck, gut loose as a bowl of cherries,
a tiny tumult rearranging in his eye.

THE AVENUE

They found a man in the shrub that shields our lane –
one fat white hand not tucked in the pit –
and cordoned off a patch. We had nothing to explain it

but *The Post*. And now the ground's re-strewn with tins
and crisp bags; sleet jiggles the ivy; the blackbirds
bob from floor to bole as each dull dusk settles in.

And coming back at night we get on too,
quickening to the safety lights, through
shadows of gates that thrust across the grit.

DRIVING THROUGH THE PIT TOWN

There's not much round here now, you say,
just huddled brick or pebbledash terraces,
and tiny new-builds where the pitheads were.

Bare hills fly up beyond the town you left,
with clasps of scree, caps of sodden green,
pitched above the neat slate pitches

but your eyes stay on the road. The side streets jut
left and right, so many of them, like ribs.
You jab a finger: *We lived up top of that one.*

Then – surprise – a pale sun picks at a slit
in the paper sky. Yellow slaps down
momently and slides along the valley,

and the half-a-pit-wheel trenched in the roundabout
shimmers, red as flesh. We won't stop here
and most of the shops – Kebabland, USA Nail's,

Milan Fashions – are shut or boarded anyway.
The four lads pincering fags outside the Co-op,
gobbing and shoving, repulse for what they are.

It's no use knowing better, more, you say.
And in blue spray paint, the back of the village sign
cries DING DONG!! like we're waiting at a door.

· 2013 ·

11

The colliery's a country park:
  his old man shunted coal.
This young dad teaches his lad to fish
  at a bug-flecked winding hole
while opposite a brace of fish
  repeats between the reeds.
'Like this,' he bellows, hands on shoulders
  pulling the kid around,
who grimaces and squares his shoulders,
  wanting the world to know
he knows. May petals file across
  in fuddles of sun-dried snow.

ANDERBY CREEK

for Ian

I went east by south-east
to the place, found everything
was there just as they'd said:
the one road leading out

and leading in: an empty beach-house,
brittle dunes, a few groynes
sloping down into the sea.

IAN PARKS, 'ANDERBY CREEK'

I heard you read this tonight in central Leicester
in a strip-lit hall as phosphorescence swelled
unseen along that coast, dimly glittering,
and slathering the groynes. Clench your eyes and gaze
distantly through the lids: it swims like that.
The hills and tight walls of your Yorkshire mining town
can recede beyond distance.

I tried to find the reason why I came.

Did it help that nothing is here?
The pub stays bolted; Skegness isn't so far
but barely smudges the night. The stars are sharp.
The place won't care if you come back. Come back.
Watch patternless algae thrash against that dark,
creating what a flailing thought makes there –
like your father lowering swiftly through the bedrock.

Aggregate din from cutlery, coffee machines
and resolute voices thickens the sweetened air
in the Eden Project Visitor Centre Café.
A red-mopped toddler slaps her Looney Tunes spork
across the high-chair table-top and stubs
her stub of hand, setting off the usual
siren of anguish. Child, the world is not
as anyone expects. My wife and I
sit several tables away, as far as we can,
and grimace as mummy lifts, with studied grace,
the utensil her progeny clutches, bringing out
a fresher growl of grief.
                              You won't remember
suffering here – or all that's yet to come
throughout this erstwhile clay pit of stinky shrubs
and leaf-dense biomes skulking the valley beyond:
two caterpillars riddled with human mites
where ice creams wait! a bamboo xylophone waits!
and I think *What could our life be*
with someone else in it?
then *You would be our life.*
                              The child shrieks on –
still hoping for all to come right? And now a waitress
totters across, all baby-smiles and hair-bun
shining on her crown, and limbs and lashes –
two thirds my age – and clears their plates, and smiles,
which stuns the infant, who softens into a stare,
head bobbling. My wife chisels her rock cake
with a knife, leaves me the bigger half,
and I set to, scrawling postcards to my parents:
an only child must remember more.
Each while, my mother hopes for news.

Each while, my father, elsewhere, hopes for news.
Will none of us say the things we've thought
until there isn't time? I'll harden my thought.
We are too many. We haven't seen enough.

Where all is water:
greening the hillside,
browning tracks

and rollicking as one
round valley-floor farms
in its endless thread.

Sheep were scattered
as expected, minding
themselves; the great

aviary of a Welsh valley
whirred and chirruped
its fragmented continuum.

In the nearest field,
a boiler-suited farmer
in miniature waddled

to an orange bucket,
threw the contents
over a thin hedge.

But only us up there,
alone and quiet,
together and separate

until I snagged her gaze.
'Do you ever want children?'
And was it being in this

over-fertile ridiculous *cwm*
made me ask it?
And neither quite said no –

watched suddenly
by the person
we won't make happen.

His bell tent has
re-birthed him and his flask
into this;

his legs stretch
to the folding bay,
the folds of Islay,

the half-folded
herring gull
and kittiwake

skirmishing
to/from
water/air.

His hands flap
go back.
He stares. Out

there, grey rock,
greyer water;
somewhere behind

the needy child, the
mortgaged flat,
the lonely wife

he forgot
to love,
the shop-floor life.

Each midge scribbles
stars over him,
bays for blood.

His hands flap
go back.
He stares out.

They aren't here of course
he's alone by the Mere
and it's years since she wanted
his child and he left
but he knows she's had babies –
then here comes the rush of
the dream of his daughter
cobbing stale breadcrumbs
at pochards and mallards
that pull handbrake turns
on the slow bunching water
before it spills tan
from the lip of the weir.

It was their first full week of being back together
in however many months. And, despite the weather,
they treated it just like a holiday.
Or she did. He was bored, annoyed, until the end of that final day
when it was too late, when they pulled into the station car park
and he unloaded the case and walked her to the barrier, his mother,
who then became a part of one train like any other,
which sighed into the dark.

They're both down by 9
  at table 5 – the

  bay window table! –
clicking cutlery

with the egg smells, clicks,
  scrapes and tiny talk,

  talking and scraping
at full Englishes.

The year dismantles
  against our wishes;

  he sees it over
her head, through warped glass:

dry leaves quave, pitch, or
  tousle ragged lawns.

  In here, buff lights burn,
the year dismantles,

and she pours coffee
  for herself, then him.

  There isn't enough.
Grains ride down the lip:

she doesn't see them,
  dark light is burning,

the year dismantles.
'It's nice here!' she says

meaning something else
it would hurt to say.

COMING OF AGE

for Emily

My tent enhanced the world it hid:
cow piss drumming the clotty soil
in sudden thrums; a moped now,
snarling round a curve in the road
behind the field-end, over the brow –
then near-silence (offset by you,
cold earring bumping across my face,
our groundsheet slipping against the dew).
Put my knees up? Leave them down?
What would someone better do?

My first real fuck, not mutual grope,
and keen to take it in, somehow,
in spite of one too many Harp
and being a little too young to cope,
I felt a kinship with that cow,
a oneness with the dampened earth
until you crab-walked off my chest,
said 'It's not working', turned and left,
jeans in hand, said 'Sorry' too loud
but left the porch door half-unzipped.

And I'd not thought about that trip
to Castlegregory again
for several months, and then it dawned
that that night I'd not put one on
so I took my girlfriend to Clinic 10
at Lincoln County and, hand on hand,
she did her best to comfort me
before we learned nothing was wrong
and I didn't care for her much again –
until she found another man.

GRANATTRICHTER MIT BLUMEN (1924)

after an etching by Otto Dix

Because he couldn't forget it eight years later
we stand ten yards from that crater,
prevented from gazing into the heart:
he blacked that in, and held us back from it.

And he recalled the background bare, but etched a chain
of full-grown wildflowers patting hands at the rim.
We know they've filled it all in, that ninety ploughs
have dragged their fingers against his remembered earth.

1.

Thirteen summers for this! At the kissing gate
she stopped and giggled simply; I didn't wait
but shimmied through – then saw it all too late
and kicked at some open-eyed daisies. Self-derision
thumped at me for days. It came in swells.
She missed my frequent calls, our second date,
and went for Paul. All week I hardly ate,
then watched them hand in hand at our village fête;
and Bosnia took up the television,
as though to mock my suffering as well.

2.

'And down at last into this lap of stone
Between four cataracts of rock.'

LAWRENCE DURRELL (1912–1990), 'SARAJEVO'

Like Lincoln (well, almost): the road north to Sarajevo
slips down a shrubby hill and suddenly we're here
in a neatened muddle of terracotta and concrete
and domes and masts, with feral dogs round the dumpsters
that snap steaming bin bags, shying from heat-slowed tourists.

A waiter swipes crumbs from our table outside Cafe Željo,
smiles down, locks eyes to warn us: 'Please watch your things –
Gypsies', he says, pulling a hand down a finger.
I hold my pocket; she touches her wedding ring.

Then we saunter in cooling evening through Baščaršija
under taut awnings, new-whitewashed uplit minarets
like rockets to God: cash in a wiped-clean city
that was bulletins when identical munitions
to the souvenir ammo – the bullet-pens, toy helicopters

from mortar shells, that we catch ourselves thinking
crass, or unnecessary – found a quoin,
a cupola, a father shivering at a standpipe,
a door-jamb, an old woman buying cigarettes.

KRUJË

'Skanderbeg's town' – and
there he is, terrible on his
plinth-top horse by the bankomat,
flanked by bee-lining stray dogs.

Where is the nearest button-shaped
Hoxha bunker? Look in be quick.
It is waist-deep in a wash
of soil and cigarette butts; and

all is as promised:

each knackered Mercedes
or Audi bucks at the corner,
throws tails of dust
to the empty sky where

the castle tower sticks
from its clifftop, like a flexed digit.
Did we come to be different –
in and apart – and find it?

REUNION

The road out of town is patchy with heat-haze
that wafts from the tarmac. Each limp little flag
drops stripes at the ground. A red barn and silo
stand guarding some corn, with a scarecrow in rags

whose head has been ripped; then a dapple of woods
and a house every while, each drive cutting down
to the road by a square of plaid green or once-green;
then houses more frequently, then the next town

where the signs saying Bernie have mostly been pulled.
Some Hillary ones have appeared in their stead.
At Union Grill, Trump v. Clinton plays out
on a muted TV, till it's cut. We break bread

and the jowly man wearing a DON'T BLAME ME! pin badge
blames England for Brexit and tells me he's 'Scotch'
but don't speak up and spoil the fun
when you know it would anger the family: 'Watch

your mouths, no politics!' our hostess has yelled,
so I pour his Bass slowly to leave a small head
and we gab through a full live-long hour until home time
then I pump his hot hand, and I wish this man well.

· SUMMER 2016 ·

So I pushed like an eager pilgrim up to the shrine,
up switchbacks of calcareous rock, alternately baked
and shaded by the olives and carobs, that rock.
Then cobbles spread near the summit – a rust-lidded well
hiding in a corner – and where they flattened out
it waited with its dark door, flat white walls,
a wave of brown-tiled roof, a split rose window.
Bells clanked brightly down in the shadowed town
where cars pressed to and fro, on the verge of silence.
A butterfly bounced across. A plane hit a mountain
but slid out the other side like thread through a needle.
Forcing the handle made the shrine door screech

and the bus-stop-sized room seemed too dark. But there they were,
ready to give their blessings for my offerings:
their unfitted crowns, dull and preposterous,
toppling permanently left and right;
the slit-gapped fingers of the infant reaching
like a lost conductor, fashioned with all the care
grim duty, if not talent, could bestow
seven hundred quiet years ago;
their eyes plump, lips quarter-smiling – even the child
knowing more than you, including you;
and a space in the Perspex screen to slip my hand through
and sense love bursting fresh from a cold beige foot.

We saw the younger one first, on the curtain wall,
painfully smiling at a camera and the sun,
her black locks buoyant and pudgy shoulders bare.
And half of her party were stood about up there
with Palma's circuit board below them, all
pointing, guffawing, kissing – the business done.

So we waved at them, forgot her, carried on:
through a colonnaded walk; past dank grey cells
surprising the few to find them; into the courtyard
where we puzzled at the statue of some bard,
tried an unmarked door, straddled a cannon,
and watched our portraits quivering down the well.

Then an organ's rumble, muffled through the stone,
grew crisp as someone opened that secret door.
This place is like a wedding factory!
you joked and moved, I thought, closer to me
as another couple stepped out, their business done –
all clichés then, whatever lay in store.

meant brusquer shocks from fauna. That line of ants, say,
curving round stones, stretching off like a motorway,
those little machines tailgating this way and that way –
but veering, confused, up my landed, still unfeeling leg.

We play at being explorers, these borrowed days.
Though tonight we made it back too late, you said,
and fell asleep. Our room opens over the bay
where a lighthouse is turning its head and turning its head.

I'm where Luca prods the map: '*This* part of town
landslide to the valley in 1963.'

A stretch of rubble, tile, timber straggles down
from a cluster of leering houses, churches, palazzi.

'Life in what stayed was too bad, so everyone left'
which brings us as voyeurs this half-century later,

with studied sorrow for nearly unshakeable heft
and how it shook, to note the gullies where rainwater

still imperceptibly picks away at the cleft
under balancing Craco. 'Mel Gibson nearly bought

the whole town when they filmed *Passion of the Christ*
down there – that is where Judas Iscariot died' –

he points to a clump of olive trees. 'The price
would not be much. But rumour is he decides

it is not worth it. Now, the future of this
hill-town is much more decay.' Luca's tried

all doors, he says. A breeze turns shutters round.
He takes me to the top, to see the sea.

ST PETER'S BASILICA

for Billy and Kate

Our line is led in to the right. Devout ones mutter.
Caps come down. The air is suddenly chill
and rich. I don't, but I want to drop to a knee
and sense myself falter as you say faith can falter.

'This building's old, men made it beautiful'
I said in a nave less old, less beautiful
when I was five, or so my father has told me –
but *Deus* remains *absconditus*. Why wouldn't He be?

We step to the crossing. Up, up, like ants on a rail,
are tourists to squint at. Talk turns on feeling and duty
in Bramante, Michelangelo, Bernini:
the struggles, for love – to awe with terrible love;

the soft marble lips curled in – fear? piety? empathy;
the kissed-smooth toes on the boilerplate bronze St Peter
as selfie-sticks dance before us at the altar.
We choose to do this together, but you see lustres

I can't. Which is fine. Till the end. For good or ill,
my *offerta* slips through the slot, then clatters at clutter.
It's hardly enough yet too much. Like this gold.
Let that be.

WRIT IN WATER

'All discussion of what happened there was forbidden.'
GUARDIAN, APRIL 2013

He spent the best of three years at Camp Nama, then Balad,
though you and I and she mustn't know what he did there.

And now they twist through Venice in a gondola –
the gondolier's *brindisi* smarts ruptured brick

and Alice, his Alice, is glad just to see him sit
for twenty minutes. She rolls her cold palm past his fist,

squeezes it like a gear stick that last moment
as they arc to a jetty; and back he shifts to himself.

Of course they can't get through this. Of course she must meet
someone easy, away from this city of hearts

and masks, where both need both but can't find either.
He wedges a note in the tip jar as he departs.

These six floors stack up from our burdened street.
He fidgets and shivers and twists in what was a garret
while, deep from our casement windows, hair-bunned waitresses flit
among their flocks of parasols, and smoke and chatter thin to meet
sidling pigeons clenched to the gable-top above us.

And I study in my study. It's more than enough
to know he exists two floors above the shelf
I'm making a life on. Some nights a hooded shadow slips to our
       shared street door
then whips away, all shoulder. Beneath my shelving, my desk
coned in light, with its breezeblocks of unrecalled thought.

BÚÐIR

after Basil Bunting

*'Tourism has become the largest revenue-generating sector
in Iceland, surpassing even such stalwart giants as fishing.'*
THE REYKJAVÍK GRAPEVINE, 3 MARCH 2015

'Tourist go home THANKS.'
GRAFFITO ON A REYKJAVÍK BUS STOP

There was a village here
under the clapboard church;

lichens curled in rare sun
eat the words for no one
on an open book of stone;

behind them, Bjarnarfoss
flushes through itself
into itself
at waves of lovers;

ocean drags and winks –
and every while
the same kittiwakes,
becoming un-
becoming.

GETAWAY

The flags are high in St Peter Port:
Liberation Day is Saturday,

someone told us, and the island is flush
with bunting. We've hiked the lane from town

and round the headlands, dipping to water
then up then to water, and now we explore

a panoptical bunker that's neck-deep in gorse,
goosegrass and sorrel, the store room behind

fizzing with flies – so we turn and stare out
at gulls on each craglet defending their nests

beside a tiny heartache cove
fringed with sea foam, a lilting yacht

pinned to its heart, bright mast ticking
like a metronome. And on

the deck of that boat a radio blurts
about Mayweather Pacquiao – the letdown it was,

and the earthquake in Asia (death toll six thousand
and rising, as blocked mountain passes are cleared).

Someone clambers, hands ready, across
the foredeck, lifts like a jockey,

arches arms to a steeple, flops in
and crawls round the turning stern. My hand

knocks yours, takes it, as we scan the scrolling
sky (sun here; rain drowning Jersey)

and in-out-folding sea, still
beside the gun mount set to swivel

in iron, here, a lifetime away.

It lists beneath a sycamore
swashing in high summer leaf,
and takes a hit from underneath:
a root-knuckle bulges along the floor.

The eight loopholes have fissures, sprouting
thistles; through each, wheat is fattening.
'What's this thing *for*?' A starling sings
its wind-up song. The sun slides out.

And this taste of piss, that Fetherlite
slumped in the corner, those Holsten cans,
the markered slogan FUCKYOU!⌐⁕⁘S·DAN
do not try to answer. Might.

From this rock-jewelled ford a few safe feet from the cracking edge
of a high plain of rumpled heather, rumpling breeze, a burn
dives, re-streaking its gully – so fast, so still
round sponge-and-matchstick trees – fleet
to that distant puddle, Loch Muich, and
out by Queen Victoria's shoreline lodge:
stock stockiness in grey gables, ringed by feather pines.
She mourned down there in heavy solitude.
Up here, a meadow pipit chats and teleports
twig to twig to twig to twig to

But you can see in that lower place –
so close and soft it seems, and all ours to see whole now –
squabbling geese materialise as dots
from the shoreline, and file slick out over
that blue-black film, not needing to process why
they do so. It shines like hematite. Down-shore
two deer, in stately deportment, turn heavy heads
at a hiker, then trot up from the path to eat.
They do not know there is no stalking today.
They do not know there was stalking yesterday.

Walk near that shifting tail and maybe you'll find
the ten-foot concrete disc from the Great War
lodged in a field, behind wire and under lichens:
a deaf ear to Deutschland. And, somewhere near,
a broad barn with a cracked corrugated roof,
by piles of worn-out tyres and mouldering dung.

We stop and startle twenty blinking Friesians
who step up to the gate for us, some huffing,
some grinding belch. Who know what they can count on:
the farmer coming each morning, all clicks and whistles;
those steel bars and the sun, the sideways rain
beyond, with the field they once lay down in;

the wobbly flanks of others; them being here –
and what? One licks her nose,
a slow pink swipe across a pad of black,
then clops away; then each in turn turns off,
like lights at night: when there's nothing to fear
why unite, why stay alert? One steps askance

and arcs her tail: a pile of slop claps down,
five taps, like irregular pentameter.
Then others break off, get back to minding themselves.
Those once-high fields beyond their breezeblock walls
are pared back down to shoots, with little lakes
of standing water rimpling in the squalls,

full of jostling gulls. Beyond, a car brakes
to take the final bend, the mile to Kilnsea:
the last eked-out village, held both sides
by walls of concrete, then sand, to mark where sea
must turn. Where homesteads outstare each high tide.

NO / TTING / HAM rises with syllables parted
As the crowd spreads tiny arms and bellows it
Echoes crashing beyond the turf
Fortify the thousands in their block of light
And their echoes which wash against the city
At each rare goal tease its obliviousness

SLEEPER

You sat askance in a taxi, jolting past rush hour,
then took the sleeper home to watch your nana –
her tight mouth sunk in shrunk surprise
still, though now her eyes were shut and breath,
not how she knew you, was all she'd battle for.

Bolting past coast then cornfields, through dusk then dark
you saw it all, then filled the flip-down berth.
And stitching your in-out sleep, the wheels battered on
sending their morse over towns, under trees, along cuttings.

SOTS HOLE

He forgets the Fenland hamlet where willows slumped at a dyke
and lapped from both ends, where a ten-year-old lad on a bike
could get in an hour, without the grown-ups knowing,
and drink from his bottle on the bank, unfettered wind blowing
the fronds in loops, and the parched fields spread like bread,
as flat as sky, with the mallards coming and going...

Twenty-five years later, and he goes back
with her to that bank, leads her down that metalled cycle track
and takes her on a bench-rail, hid in a hide.
The latch would open to a world still simplified,
where willows comb water and unseen mallards meander.
And she pulls him close – all he once thought he wanted.

Back in Nocton bus stop. Opposite,
a square of light appears, and then a man
in profile, rippling behind the frosted glass,

who cleans his teeth in silence, then returns
to where he came from, returns the square to dark,
returns us to one other. Now Mike can pass

the joint he'd hidden up his sleeve. It's out.
Don't let 'im see uz! Light it be'ind the bin!
he says, so I do. It tastes a bit like meat

and though we guess we're high and still don't know
this hash we've bought's a crumbled oxo cube,
we sense it isn't really working right.

It can't be long before we'll call it a night:
there's school to barely attend the following day,
and Elly Smith, shirt-front taut like shrink-wrap,

who'll cover our folders in hearts and never like us,
and far too soon be pregnant with her first.
An on-off gust bosses the trees about

and quivers street lamps. They're stuck here just like us,
whose only knowledge of life's the best of it.
For now we'll relax, let smoking do its worst.

BETWEEN VILLAGES

for Mike

Past dusk and still it caws, slipping air,
tail out like a hand of cards,
along the pinwale field. Beyond, nothing
but plough-built ridges and furrows, ridges
and furrows full of seed and cobbles

ending by the village where we grew up.
Slung above, the Plough's slack cord of lights
is tiny in all this blackening blue –
and our galaxy, lost where I come from now,
is waiting to lift my gaze until

a light on Field-End Cottage appears,
throws flat a hedge, and a man steps out
the door beneath, and stamps off along
the bridle path: he's a torchlight jinking.
We nod in passing. Wish each other evening.

I've read the signs. Still, I hand her change –
a small rough tube of copper and silvery coins
but 'All I've got', I add. Amir's Kebabz
is yellow and empty. Miley Cyrus comes on.
Our new friend bites the pizza I gave up

two slices from the end, then starts again:
'At 9 I'm due in court for shoplifting
so I took this jumper out of H&M
to look presentable. I've got my pride,
they can't take that.' (...*we can kiss who we want*...)

'I've just made some mistakes.' 'What?' 'Alcohol.'
(...*so la da di da di*...) 'And heroin:
I've just sucked off a bloke for twenty quid.
When dad died I went mad. I lost my flat.
I lost my kids an' all.' Somewhere, something

bangs: a car? Mike gets his wallet out,
says 'Don't do that' and slips her two crisp tenners
which disappear, before she disappears,
calling a functional 'Thanks.' (...*we run things,
they don't run we*...). We stand and open the door,

which Amir (?) locks behind us. The slabs are slick
with watery streetlight, mulch, the dints of years.
A stilettoed clubber clops and lists our way.
'Let's go,' Mike says. I'm glad; he lifts a hand.
A black cab three-point-turns right where we stand.

St Denys' is making its stab for the Maker
and the 07:19 for Lincoln is rattling through its break
in the fields, then over a culvert, and on it you sit,
and look up from *Bizarre* straight through the view

where a church spire is flat on the whiteness of sky
with one dour gull shooting clear across its tip
and over the rain-bright roofs, cracked tarmac, then you,
and on to the coast where sharp groynes cut the breakers.

It's rock reconstituted on the rock,
order cut from the ground.
Three beeches sway eternally;
the path is soft with leaves
and bats wheel round and slice and swoop
from yew to nook to eave.
Over the fields a stub of moon
smudges the scudding cloud.

And an owl is pinned to that cloud, until it's not.
No screech will let you know
a kill's been made. Death is small
and practical, in the shadow
where thistles thrust their pinnacles
each way: at the hedgerow,
the Milky Way, the lop-toothed huddle
of graves, the wilted window.

And you are scattered between that window and hedge –
though who can say? Ash
is finer than earth. And as the wind
stalls and blows, you must
be shifting where the owl was pinned,
and round the yews and beeches,
pirouetting on graves, out of reach,
where dust is piled on dust.

They patter from myriad hatchbacks to sit in steam,
to rub oils in, to sluice off Moroccan muds
and come out looking the same, but feeling good
or at least not the same. A few accepting men
have joined their quiet wives for Special Days,
but teatime finds them waiting up in the gallery
where crisp skylights show off the Victorian chimneys,
the fat iron guttering embossed with dates.
And down in the pool women's heads bob past
at tiny speeds, all stern and solitary;
and farther off, in the large mosaicked Jacuzzi,
a sultry twenty-something climbs away
from the bald jolly woman full of knots and cancers
between treatments, between friends, here to feel better.

Blackberries bulge all over the bush.
Her arthritic fingers claw slowly,
hunting the ones that give, and he
looks on, accepting what he sees

and no longer gets: how as a kid on this moor
he stamped a nettle den, and ten years later
took her up this lane, behind those pines,
then brought her off by a woodpile in a rain

that weighted his shirt and numbed his back.
And had the blackberries been fat that year
he'd hardly have noticed – and have eaten more of them.
She tugs an end one from its dwindled stem,

she who's left her youth behind and faced
forward; he understands because he chose
her life, too young to know it was. He takes
her blotchy paw, and smiles, and off they go.

He was kind as could be, her grandpapa.
His heart gave out – and then gave in
weeding these beds. His blood was too thin, see.
He died on his spade – where them greengages are.

Her house, her estate, but she's never here.
I twist a greengage from its stalk
then nibble, and still you talk and talk.
And not knowing either it's hard to care,
but one mustn't let on. The beans fill their rows,
the herbs stuff their pots; air waits, and blows,

wheels free, but panders to the walls.
His rose-heads pander to that wind.
And yards above a bullfinch calls.
And miles above a satellite spins.

OPEN means almost empty, or so she finds. The heating gurgles;
traffic slogs past, its groans now dulled by windows and blinds.
She steps to some faceless mannequins, tight in their dull-bright taffeta,
then over to an oak-rimmed table cabinet, where she finds

a tersely labelled miscellany of snuff boxes, gemstones, watches –
and among it the dull wedding band her great-great-grandmother wore,
though how could she know? She taps the glass. Her spectacled eyes flit
over it, and pretty much everything else, then draw her back to the door.

LOVE IN A LIFE

'Ah, but they had each other.'
GABRIEL ARROYO, *LOS BIBLIÓFILOS*

The old suit reading the *Telegraph* at his wife
in the Quiet Coach of our train to Paddington
uncrosses his legs, cracks me with a toe,
raises the *Sorry* hand and carries on
steadily, as before. And when he says so
she leads him down the aisle and out of my life:

he hulks an alloy trolley-case from the rack
then holds her pallid hand. The engine goes slack
and others rise, putting him out of sight;
this train shunts off the train. I stretch, lean back,
and on we slide, through white and yellow lights,
then lights stretched down a river, then near-black.

From each fat coin
spindles rooted and tugged at the shore wind
and some of the tips clicked off in his small hands
like rills of wax, but it didn't matter.

Then candy floss smothered his face, its hairs in his hair
as they leaned through the gusts at the tip of the pier,
a hand in Papa's jacket pocket
scrunching his sweet-smelling cigarette packet.

Seventy years ago, that; but part of now for him
last week, when he was calling for more water,
or for Mother, too gone to understand
but still going, hard blooms blooming through the colon.

So passing wasn't to dwell on. And as
the small troop passes the home, his elm box
propping DAD in cut chrysanthemums,
the gruff sons tight to their tight-lipped mum,

the room he took shows curtain-backs to the street
and they've taken down his blinds.
And writhing from nub torsos across the sand
spindles root and tug at the shore wind.

These fifteen stones
cleave the bog like wisdom
teeth. The moor
leans over.

Then it clouded.
Then scared lambs
drummed the clearing,
their tiny tails wheeling.

And from a plot
up the opposing ridge
six hundred pines swirl lances at the sky
until the cutters come.

TUESDAY

for and about DR BOB PINTLE
Lecturer in Creativity, Peterborough University

Dedicated also to DR ANDREW TAYLOR
who did not inspire the poem

8AM: THE SNOOZE BUTTON

Life repeats – like a triolet,
thinks Bob, as the alarm clock trills,
and he starts composing this triolet.
Life repeats like a triolet:
promotion is always a book away;
the bed stays warm; the post brings bills.
And no one likes a triolet.

9AM: AVOIDING PROFESSOR McNISH

See McNish: a tweed-clad type –
an archetype – with brogues and pipe;
who knows it all, bar when to stop;
    who works on Scott;
who'll always be in the coffee shop
    when you wish he would not;

who'll say more than the subjects knew
about Blind Harry, Barbour's *Brus*;
who, spotted through the window screen,
    drives Pintle out
in futile search of a vending machine.
    Bob struts about,

comes back at twenty past, buys a cup
of mochaccino, slurps it up,
feels more himself, almost okay –
   I avoided the bore.
Then bumps straight into him anyway
   in the corridor.

10AM: THE FIRST-YEAR SEMINARS

That's thirty minutes he won't get back
   and Pintle's behind time,
climbing Arts Tower to teach a group
   on *Being and Time*.

He opens the door. The room goes quiet.
   And after about an hour
very little more's been said;
   and down at the foot of the Tower

Pintle watches those seven students
   tramp straight to the SU bar,
sighs, waits a minute, then opens the door
   for his second seminar.

2PM: THE DEPARTMENTAL MEETING

Twenty-four adults sit about on standby
as dulled as their students. The water goes round,
then the minutes from last time. The agenda goes round.

Item 1: Student Engagement: 'Each of us must strive to…'
and Pintle nods when the other ones nod
and absently scribbles a peach. Twenty-five past two.

59

Item 2: the Course Rolling Action Plan,
which strives to live up to its acronym.
A PowerPoint chart slides in. Slides out again.

Half past two. Twenty to three. Three.
Item 3: Library Update: 'The new MacAnthony Library
will have a cafe, Social Zone and Learning Pods'

'– And might get finished eventually', Professor Gunt quips.
Item 4: Student Feedback: 'Our Year One rep, Sandi,
expressed concerns about…'. *Ah, lovely, untouchable Sandi…*

3PM: DEVISING MODULES TO COMPLY WITH PU'S
NEW EMPLOYABILITY AGENDA

· Poetry that Works
· Bookkeeping for Moll Flanders
· Getting ~~the Most~~ out of ~~Being~~ Here

4PM: THE OFFICE HOURS

Second year essay tutorial slots,
A–H. And next: Sophie Cage.
'But *how* can I make it more better?', she says,
rutting her brow in effort. And rage.

The Hello Kitty rubber impaled on her pencil
gawps eagerly, bobbing above the page
as she jots bubble-lettered misspelled iterations
of his battle to seem at once honest and sage.

Though empathy is not his strength,
Pintle knows a brute impasse

when he sees one. This is his tenth
year at PU, and tomorrow's task –
now havocking him – is his Annual Review:
What have you done? What will you do?
How many items did you publish this year?
(But no one asking what they are.)
Is your 'Guarantee Not to Strike' with HR?

He talks on at Sophie, but isn't quite here,
and down in the quad some students clutch hands,
or frown at *The Remains of the Day* –
and each represents forty grand
to the bastards who set Pintle's pay.

ACKNOWLEDGEMENTS

Some of these poems have appeared, occasionally in slightly different versions, in *Archipelago*, *The Dark Horse*, *The Hopkins Review*, *The Interpreter's House*, *Magma*, *The Manchester Review*, *New Statesman*, *PN Review*, *Poetry*, *Poetry Review*, *The Times Literary Supplement*, and *Under the Radar*. I am very grateful to the editors of these publications, and to Nicholas Friedman, Alan Jenkins and William Ivory for reading the typescript.